THE YALE DRAMA SERIES

David Charles Horn Foundation

The Yale Drama Series is funded by the generous support of the David Charles Horn Foundation, established in 2003 by Francine Horn to honor the memory of her husband, David. In keeping with David Horn's lifetime commitment to the written word, the David Charles Horn Foundation commemorates his aspirations and achievements by supporting new initiatives in the literary and dramatic arts.

Celia, a Slave

BARBARA SEYDA

Foreword by Nicholas Wright

Yale UNIVERSITY PRESS   NEW HAVEN & LONDON

Set in ITC Galliard and Sabon types by Integrated Publishing Solutions.
Printed in the United States of America.

Library of Congress Control Number: 2016932439
ISBN 978-0-300-19706-8 (pbk : alk. paper)

A catalogue record for this book is available from the British Library.

This paper meets the requirements of ANSI/NISO Z39.48–1992 (Permanence of Paper).

10 9 8 7 6 5 4 3 2 1

Contents

Foreword

*C*elia, a Slave was chosen as winner of the 2015 Yale Drama Series Award by myself and a panel of twelve. Francine Horn, who is the originator and presiding genius of the David Charles Horn Foundation, had asked me to judge the competition for a period of two years, taking over from the American playwright Marsha Norman. (Judges are appointed biennially and alternately from the United States and the United Kingdom.)

Between fourteen and fifteen hundred entries had arrived, far more than I could deal with myself, so I assembled a panel of twelve people I knew and trusted: the playwrights Alice Birch, Howard Brenton, Rebecca Lenciewicz, and Barney Norris; the directors Natalie Abrahami, Jeff James, and Amelia Sears; the dramaturges Tom Lyons (National Theatre) and David Tushingham (Dramaturg Salzburg Festival); the Royal Court artistic associate Emily McLaughlin; the former Channel Four commissioning editor Peter Ansorge, and the Faber editorial director of drama Dinah Wood. Each of us took as many plays as we thought we could handle, and between us we assessed them all.

Two meetings followed: one where we introduced our favorite plays and argued for them, sometimes successfully and sometimes not; and a second meeting around my kitchen table, where we talked through the twelve short-listers that all of us had read.

Our discussions were uninhibited, serious, funny, and generous. A few of the panelists were almost as old as me, and I'm in my seventies; most were in their twenties or barely out of them. I was intrigued by the coincidences of opinion (many) and the differences (hardly any) that occurred across the generations.

I was also struck by the difference between choosing plays for production—which I've been involved in for much of my life—and judging them for a competition. If the aim is production, then all sorts of other factors start raising their heads, some prosaic, some verging on the ignoble. Can we afford to do a play with such an enormous cast? Can we find the right director? How well will this play sit in the program, when you view the program overall? Will it clash?

Judging plays for a competition is a purer craft, though it's not always easy to define what one is doing. You're look-ing for a good play, no two ways about that. The question that nags is, What constitutes "good"? Is it a subjective view that grows on you for reasons you can't define? Or a cool assessment of how successful you think the play would be if it were produced? Or should you measure the play against a set of rules? "Well-rounded characters (6), lucid storytelling (8), satisfactory resolution (4)"?

(This last method is more common than you might think. I've quite often seen plays judged by their success or failure to observe a set of formulas that don't have any existence except in the head of the person doing the judging. As the prospect of production is alluring for the writer, this causes a lot of rewriting to take place, though few plays are much improved by it. Mostly they simply become more like other plays.)

The truest reaction is the absence of doubt. You start to read and the play takes over. It catches you up, it sweeps you along, the strings of your heart begin to stir in sympathetic

vibration, and you reach the last page in a state of extraordi-
nary good cheer: you know that the ancient human genius
for creating deep metaphor out of observed reality is still
alive. This happens rarely: when I was reading plays daily
at the National Theatre, once a year was about as much as I
could hope for.

Reading plays below this stratospheric level constitutes
work, but it's work of a very rewarding kind. Few people
believe this, but nobody ever started reading a play without
hoping that it would be good. If that hope dies, it's because
the play has killed it by some word or action or development
that you don't believe, belief being the essential test.

Do you believe the characters? Not just "believe" in the
sense of finding them roughly lifelike: that's setting the bar
too low. Can you hear their voices? Do you find yourself
reading their words aloud? Can you see the characters in
your mind's eye? Can you see their surroundings? Reading
plays, just like producing them or acting in them, is an in-
tensely sensuous business: colors, voices, and physical sensa-
tions are an intimate part of it.

What else are you looking for? Originality, of course: *orig-
inal* in the sense that the basis of the play is life as opposed
to art. Personality: the sense that the play is written by a
human being and not a machine. You look for life, meaning
enough buoyancy to keep the action in the air. And to my
eye at least, what comes tops is the humane element. This
isn't dowdy naturalism: it's the ability to convey the intelli-
gence, empathy, and sparkle that makes us human. "What a
piece of a work is a man," says Hamlet the prince, extolling
God's creation of humanity. Whenever I see this scene, I
imagine a kind of shadow-drama in which Shakespeare is
caught marveling at his power to create astonishing people.
And his acknowledgment of failure: "And yet, to me, what is
this quintessence of dust?"

When I read a play, I try to act as a blank screen, sensitive
to whatever is being beamed at it: the play-reading equiva-

lent of a psychoanalyst. I don't talk back, as it were, and I try not to let my artistic, political, or moral prejudices affect my judgment. But as my prejudices, like everyone else's, are invisible to me, I've no way of knowing how successful I'm being at putting them aside. I was reminded of this yesterday when I read the words of a British Asian poet writing about the lack of cultural diversity in British publishing: "If you think you're liberal-minded and, therefore, fair- and open-minded, you're probably the most dangerous person for minority writers; you probably think your taste is broadly representative and takes the middle ground."

I can't logically argue against this, but it's a good cue to point out a couple of things about the Yale competition.

One is that the plays are read blind. Neither the panel nor the judge has any way of knowing the name of the writer, or of his or her sex or heritage. I occasionally asked the rest of the panel whether they thought that such-and-such a play had been written by a man or a woman. The general answer was the same as the answer that I would have given: they hadn't thought about it.

The other is that entries are positively encouraged from anyone who feels that he or she has the ability to write a play. A lot of competitions concentrate on entries from theaters, agents, and literary managers, with the result that they're less welcoming to people from outside a theatrical charmed circle. There's an element of natural democracy about the Yale system, and it's something I like enormously.

The panel and I narrowed our choices to a final three: Craig Thornton's *The High Cost of Heating*, a brilliantly imaginative two-hander in which a very ordinary married couple is overwhelmed by the utility and other bills assailing them to the extent of actually snaking their way up through the toilet; Abe Koogler's austere and observant *Kill Floor*, which by coincidence was produced in fall 2015 at Lincoln Center; and this one.

But it was *Celia, a Slave* that finally won, through the mus-

cularity of its language, the vivid individuality of its characters, and the intensity of the grief it evoked. It was much later
that the author was revealed to us as Barbara Seyda, a woman
experienced in many aspects of the theater, though never before as the author of a play, living in Tucson, Arizona.

Nicholas Wright

Celia, a Slave

Location: Fulton Jail cell, Callaway County, Missouri

Time: Eve of Celia's execution, December 20, 1855.
The hanging, December 21, 1855, 2 pm.

Note: At age 19, Celia, a female slave, was accused, convicted
and hanged for killing her 66-yr.-old master, Robert Newsom,
a prosperous Missouri landowner. This play is based on the
trial transcript and court records from *The State of Missouri vs.
Celia, a Slave,* File #4496, Callaway County Court, Fulton
Township, Missouri, 1855. The play is a tableau of interviews
with the dead.

One of the following newspaper articles may be projected,
as the audience enters the theater: "Fiendish Murder Near
Fulton, Mo." Reprint from *Missouri Republican,* the *New York
Times,* July 2, 1855, or "Hanging a Negress," reprint from
Fulton Telegraph, the *New York Times,* January 16, 1856.

Play runs without an intermission.

Cast of Characters
(in order of appearance)

VIOLA Slave woman. 30 yrs. old. Lives on Powell farm.

MILDRED LOUISA ROLLINS 82 yrs. old. White, upper class. Sister of James Sidney Rollins.

BETHENA An elder. Free woman of color. 80 yrs. old.

POLLY NEWSOM 19 yrs. old. Daughter of Robert Newsom.

ULYSSES, a.k.a. UNCLE PEE WEE Enslaved man of color. 75 yrs. old. Insane asylum inmate.

COFFEE WAYNESCOT 11 yrs. old. Robert Newsom's grandson. Virginia's son.

SOLACE Runaway slave. Street griot.

DAVID NEWSOM Robert Newsom's son. 22 yrs. old.

AUNT WINNIE 26-yr.-old St. Louis slave. Accordion player.

JUSTICE ABIEL LEONARD Missouri Supreme Court justice.

MATT 10-yr.-old slave boy on Death Row. Celia's cellmate.

WILLIAM POWELL 41-yr.-old neighbor of Robert Newsom. Farmer, slaveowner.

GEORGE   22-yr.-old enslaved male. Celia's lover.

DR. HOCKLEY YOUNG   Physician called by state to testify at
Celia's trial.

VIRGINIA WAYNESCOT   36 yrs. old. Robert Newsom's
daughter. Has 4 children.

VINE   5 yrs. old. Slave. Celia's daughter.

BENJAMIN SHEETS   Juror. One of 12 white male jurors on
Celia's trial.

JOHN JAMESON   Celia's defense attorney. 53-yr.-old white
male. Slaveowner.

EUPHRATES   Midwife. 40 yrs. old. Delivers Celia's 3rd child
in jail.

JUDGE WILLIAM AUGUSTUS HALL   Circuit Court judge.
U.S. senator. Slaveowner.

HIGGLER   Hangman.

FELIX BARTEY   Callaway Circuit Court clerk.

CELIA   19-yr.-old slave. Convicted and sentenced to death.

ANNOUNCEMENT: Celia, a Slave. Location: Fulton Jail Cell, Callaway County, Missouri. Time: Eve of Celia's execution, December 20, 1855. This play is based on the trial transcript and court records from the *State of Missouri vs. Celia, a Slave*, File #4496, Callaway County Court, Fulton Township, Missouri, 1855. The play is a tableau of interviews with the dead.

CAST *enters as a force field. A magma chamber erupting with pent-up emotion, resentments, epiphanies. Banging and burst through both doors at the front of the house. Rowdy and volatile. Yelling staggered fragments of text. Physically agitated. Eviscerate the space.* VIOLA *is the last to enter.* CAST *climbs onstage, aggressive and belligerent. Takes seats. Lights out. Play begins.* VIOLA *downstage center speaks.*

3 fragments for each character, yelled simultaneously and overlapping.

VIOLA   Eyes like a demon. A dagger in my heart. Twelve copper bathtubs.

MILDRED   She drank pickle juice. Imagine that! Garish and utterly burlesque.

BETHENA   No-count white rattlesnake. Go get that old ruffian. Roughnecks and perverts.

POLLY   Children of Christ Almighty. O beloved father. My hair is a cyclone.

COFFEE   Use some grease, boy! Grandpa was fornicatin'. Mealworm beetles.

SOLACE   You could be a witch. She stabbed him 96 times. Shit, that ain't nothin'.

DAVID   Erroneous identification of the crime scene. Fifty yards from the main house. Our hog man got rebellious.

JUSTICE LEONARD   Sycophants and scavengers. My silk handkerchiefs. An extravagant gala.

MATT   Ain't no sugar bowl. I'm bushwackin'. Grit her teeth.

WILLIAM   Vicious nigger bitch. 'Fess up girl. Killin' is killin'.

GEORGE   Deci'mate him. Quit that old man. What'd I just say?

DR. YOUNG   The entire burnt corpse. 1100 degrees Celsius. Sexual deviancy.

VIRGINIA   Hatful of assholes. There's a rat that needs killin'. Squealin' like a pig.

VINE   A big ol' giant. They had guns. Mama was cryin'.

BENJAMIN   Licentious, pernicious fornicatress. Shady belly-cheatin' gizzard. A boil on my butt.

JOHN   She was lynched. A circus of injustice. A scorpion girt by fire.

EUPHRATES   Cold as a grave digger's butt. Drop that baby in a coal bucket. Dey sold dat chile.

JUDGE HALL   The defendant had no right. Under Missouri law. The crucible of slavery.

HIGGLER   Bloody cunt. Defecation. Kidney, livers and tripe.

FELIX   171 days. Sixty-eight dollars and forty cents. The most horrible tragedy.

CELIA   I was born bad. Reeky, thick-eyed rat-catcher. Got yanked up.

VIOLA *A slave woman. Thirty years old. Lives on Powell farm, neighbor to Newsoms.*

Massa Powell shot a woman through the head.
Threw her to the hounds.
Da buzzards ate her up.
'Cuz she run away.
Missus ain't no angel.
Eyes like a demon.
Viper in a swamp.
She say, Don't run your tongue.
Ah hope your baby is dead.
'Cuz were a crime for a slave to tell who the father of her child *was*.
See dose horses runnin' in the field.
Appaloosas, palominos.
They born free and run wild.
Belong to no one.
Except on dis earth and under da sky.
Yes'm.
Hummingbird comes to da hibiscus.
Bittersweet morning glory.
Honeysuckle.
Dey got ruby-painted necks.
Tiniest birds y'all ever did see.
Wings battin' so quick.
Emerald-like green.
And boy, does they love dose flowers.
Dat climber, hangin' heavy over the trellis.
Like nectar in heaven.
Wisteria and da lilacs.

Fall like diamond chandeliers.
Sweetness and honey.
All dat perfume in da air.
Make me feel like a wild gazelle.
Oh yes, ah intend to buy my freedom.
Ah wants to be free.
Under da law.
Yes'm.
Scripture says oppression makes even a wise man mad.
Proclaim liberty to the captive.
Unleash them that are bound.
Ah'm a slave woman and ah's got a dagger in my heart.
Massa and missus decide my fate.
Colored gal down here years before me.
She old and starvin'.
So hungry she stole a chicken and was cookin' it.
Massa Powell irate, he found out some way.
Force her eat it while it boilin'. She got scalded.
Died right away. Burnt her insides out.
Glory be to the hummingbird and the horse.
What does freedom mean for our people?
Us colored.
Dey's a colored aris'tocracy in St. Louis.
Barber named Cyprian Clamorgan.
Has twelve copper bathtubs.
Prince of Wales got shaved there.
And a St. Louis lady. Brown-skinned, straight haired.
'Bout fifty.
Miss Pelagie Rutgers.
Live on Seventh Street. In a mansion.
She bought her freedom for three dollars.
Now she own a piano dat cost two thousand dollars,
and a whole block of houses.
She worth half a million dollars.
Infinite mercy!

MILDRED LOUISA ROLLINS   *82 years old. White, affluent, upper class. From Columbia, Missouri. Katharine Hepburn–ish. Attending the Campbells' Christmas party in St. Louis.*

Lord love a duck!
Due to precocious senility, I can't remember what I ate for breakfast this morning.
I do recall one thing-a-ma-bob.
The allegedly elite society will be at the Campbells' Christmas party tonight.
All the hotsy-totsy women undulating like jellyfish in their corsets.
Like a pantheon of fat prostitutes knitting.
Boasting about their husbands and snubbing each other over who made the most delectable eclairs and tea cakes.
Last Christmas, a vixen in a silk dress, high boots and long, blood-red nails carried a pail of live eels.
She sat there, plunging her hand into the squirming eels and smiling.
Some of the older grande dames sat like half-dead catfish wearing molted turkey and pigeon feathers.
In a migrating state of entropy.
Deranged long mouths sucking on plum candy, sitting on leather couches.
Gargoyles,
garish and utterly burlesque.
I'd rather stay home.
Sip tea from a carved bowl made from a human skull.
Oh they're all right—or all rotten.
Octopi with cinched waists.

Upright female sponges and exotic slime.
They keep their chin up a bit so they have to look down at
you.
It's like being in an exclusive high-brow purgatory.
Orange lips float unattached to their tray of sins.
It's a morbid spectacle.
Irridescent reindeer.
Taxidermy elves.
A glowing statue of Eros, a sterling-silver harp.
Nameplates mounted on each deer.
A towering tree emblazoned and dripping with
unusual blown-glass ornaments, like a young girl holding a
basket
of apples wearing knickers, wings and a pair of menacing
horns.
Never know who will show up.
Zachary Taylor, U.S. military generals, or George Caleb
Bingham.
Joseph W. Postlewaite and his Free Colored Orchestra.
Or Aunt Winnie and her accordion
playing waltzes, mazurkas, schottisches, quadrilles,
marches,
and the St. Louis quick-step.
Oh, Mrs. Campbell's Roman punch always thrills the
guests.
Rinds of 24 lemons, 8 oranges, 4 pounds of sugar.
Two bottles of champagne and the whites of 16 eggs beaten
to a *stiff* froth.
And most predictably, a batch of divine homemade bathtub
gin for your tasting delight!
What else?
A golden leopard sitting on a roasted wild boar
in castles of baked meat.
Venison, woodcock, swan, geese, quail, partridge, roasted
mallard.
A civet of hare.

Delicate tarts.

Amber jelly.

A sphinx sculpted of sugar and meringue.

Perhaps a swarm of live peacock.

I'm going with my brother James Sidney Rollins, the
founder of the University of Missouri.

He's a lawyer and senator.

He taught law at Harvard.

This house is a sort of museum.

See this chair.

It's the penitentiary rocker.

James Sidney heard the petition of a prisoner-to-be.

The guards wanted to cut off his beard.

James said it would be like losing a part of his life.

They spared him a shave.

In appreciation, the inmate—in bearded gratitude—built
this chair.

Not the upholstery.

I commissioned that.

Boy, that chair needs dusting.

Just yesterday, James Sidney sold four slaves on the steps of
the courthouse.

One of them a 12-year-old, another 17, as part of an estate
sale.

But he declared quietly to me, "Slavery cannot be defended
either upon moral or religious grounds
or upon principles of natural right or political economy."

He *is* one of Boone County's largest slaveowners.

Owns 138 slaves himself.

That's a smorgasbord.

And his carriage driver, Ulysses Harney, landed in the Fulton Lunatic Asylum.

James had him committed as a person of unsound mind.

As verifiably insane.

The first colored inmate.

Mother, peering down from heaven, or looking up from
hell,
used to brag that James had no black mistresses.
Which makes me think he only has white mistresses.
Why on earth?
How did she know that?
It's quite acceptable, men and their mistresses.
All is forgiven.
But a woman!
Well, it's inconceivable.
An adulteress would be burned alive.
Or eaten by wolves.
Mother was a self-declared snob.
She drank pickle juice with gin.
A sophisticate.
Darling must have felt inadequate, don't you think?
She descended from a previous generation of socialites,
lawyers, university professors,
and snobs.
I believe she always felt superior—or inferior—to everyone.
My father, Curtis Burson Rollins, grew up on a dairy farm.
He'd say, "You can whip our cream. But you can't beat our
milk."
Once they had a two-headed calf born on the farm.
Calf must go with the cow.
But the mother rejected the strange creature.
Farmers came from miles around to see the circus cow.
Imagine that!
Miraculously, my dear brother, James Sidney, is very brainy.
He has a genius mind and what is believed to be a photo-
graphic memory.
Read law in the office of Abiel Leonard,
recent appointment to the Missouri Supreme Court.
Leonard just ruled on that case in Fulton.
The State of Missouri vs. a female slave.

Now that colored girl's in a dilly of a pickle.
A predicament.
I'm absolutely appalled.
Murder has a curious way of clearing the decks.
Old fleshmonger patriarch had his—indiscretions.
Lord love a duck!
I heard Mr. Newsom's funeral back in June was—
well, there was no open casket.
No casket at all.
He was just a hoo-hoo.
A fart in a windstorm.
A pile of dust and ashes.
I said, well, Newsom's saved money there.
Keep your hair on.
Funeral bill of sale:
The casket, handles and plate cost 150 dollars.
30 dollars for the slate vault.
10 dollars for embalming the body.
6 dollars for opening the grave.
24 dollars for the coach and pallbearers.
9 dollars for the wagon ride.
Also, 8 dollars for a new shirt.
5 dollars for the clergyman.
Well, the Newsoms, they saved 242 dollars.
Marvelous!

BETHENA   *An elder. Free woman of color. About eighty years old.*

Can't pull the wool over my eyes.
I see the evil root.
Worst rot. Plat-footed, hackle-ass old son of a bitch.
That's a white man's child. Lord's truth.
I can have the law on anyone that put a hand on me.
He on his way to the fires of hell and torment.
Ain't worth the dirt under my feet.
Burnt old boot. Egg-suckin' dog. Chewed up. Nasty.
Stinkin'. Low-down. No-count white rattlesnake.
Pestiferous tyrant. Piece of bestiality. Vulgar money bags.
Shot pouch longer than the barrel.
Newsom is an evil fool.
Even a dead fool.
Vengeance is mine, saith the Lord. You going to pay.
A penalty has to be paid.
Fat slick ridin' albino.
Grind him into sausage.
Swindler. Smilin' rat bastard.
Smelly old dead magistrate.
You get that no-shit lowlifer outta my corn. You hear me?
You is marked.
He knew what he was doing.
White folks love to keep these uppity characters alive.
But blood and lies won't kill the soul of the slave.
Evil lives close to the heart.
Give him up.
Go get that old ruffian. Useless rogue. Dead, rottin, maggot-eatin' ogre.

Give 'em to the devil.

Grievous, mendacious, concealed sins. No shit.

White man sick with his own corruption and decay.

Atonement takes many forms. Ah say it again. Atonement takes many forms.

Prediction number one. George will run and then be taken down.

Prediction number two. Harry Newsom will disallow Celia to see her own children.

And three. There's a nigger in the woodpile.

Oh yeah. Who told you about that? Who told you? Give it up.

I never 'sociates wit' trashy people, white or colored.

Filthy dealin' stash-splitter white slaveowner. You is. Ain't 'chuh?

Take this goofer dust, some red pepper, cat hair, dog tooth, salt, gunpowder.

One dried, one-eyed toad, old lizard, wing of a bat, eyes of a cat, liver of an owl.

Heart of a hawk. Or a rooster. Wrap it up. Put it under the hawthorn tree. Den cast yer spell. Put a hex on that whole family.

What you thinkin'? Dey don't deserve it?

Ah ain't got nothin' but the truth here.

Brick Willis of Boonville disappeared years ago in a puff of blue smoke.

Was beaten in a conjuratin' contest.

Wife of St. Louis voodoo sold his soul to Satan.

She sellin' charms, tellin' fortunes and misfortunes. Find lost spirits.

Spew venom remedies.

Yes, they is Negro Voodooism.

Faith-healin' rituals and spells to invoke vengeance.

Court give out no punishment for the crimes.

Rampant injustice.

Batterin' of black and mulatto females by white men.

Repeat dis spell over da fire:

Negress Sylvia. Died November 16, 1813. Legs chained. St. Louis County.

Julie Labaddie. Died November 5, 1818. Head beaten and injured. St. Louis County.

Slave Fanny. Died July 1, 1826. Injury unknown. Pike County.

Slave Annice. Died April 24, 1826. Whipping. Cape County.

Slave Patience. Died January 6, 1829. Whipping. Washington County.

Slave Delphia. Died February 2, 1830. Whipping. St. Louis County.

Slave Dinah. Died October 29, 1833. Whipping. Clay County.

Slave Hannah. Died June 27, 1834. Whipping. St. Louis County.

Slave Rachael. Died March 13, 1842. Whipping. Saline County.

Slave Minerva. Died July 24, 1842. Head beaten with an ax. Montgomery County.

Slave Sarah. Died August 13, 1847. Whipping and starved. Clark County.

Slave Aliza. Died November 13, 1860. Clubbed, axed, choked, throat slit, poisoned and shot. Boone County.

What is the outcome? Punishment for the slaveholders?

Nothin'.

Two months in jail. One-hundred-dollar fine.

Dey's brutal.

Rancid, ferocious, treacherous roughnecks and perverts.

You not gonna sit yer tail there.

I'm gonna kick your ass, boy.

Knock yer damn brains out.

POLLY NEWSOM   *19 years old. Daughter of Robert New-*
som. Living in the main house. Born November 2, 1836. 10th
of Newsom's 12 children.

What am I wearing to the hanging?
A confectionary hat.
Made of sugar.
Cream and scarlet with orange-dyed ostrich feathers.
Covered with pearlescent frosting. Sequins.
My chalky pockmarked face and the hat shall be painted.
Like a holiday cake.
With a canopy of stars rearranged in unexpected ways.
Hypnotic constellations.
Perhaps turquoise or green?
Which color fancies you?
My sister Julia arrived yesterday from Brown County,
Kansas.
Father considered Julia the "smart" one.
She became a schoolteacher.
And at the age of twenty, she fell in love with a young man,
Thomas Reynolds.
But Father would not give his consent.
He thought Julia was too intelligent for such a marriage.
So then, Rebecca became enamored with him.
She is the "beauty" of the family. Married him in 1838.
Now comes the real shocker!
Four years later, Julia had a baby by this man. Her own
brother-in-law.
About 1842. And another baby the following year.
We all disowned her.
We're a fine Christian family.

Dear brother Harry's the only one who spoke to her.

O God. 'Tis thy prerogative to kill, to cure, to wound, to heal, and wilt Thou bless my dear

sister, through life and finally save her in heaven for the Great Redeemer's sake?

In 1850, same year Celia arrived, Julia moved to Brown County.

Married William S. Williams. The "S" standin' for "Savage."

Had six more children and raised over half million bushels of corn.

But she's back for the hangin'.

Sally Boggs is stayin' with us.

Sally says we Newsoms came from France.

About 1066 during the invasion of England by William the Conqueror.

Imagine that!

Later some Newsoms were with Washington in the Revolutionary War.

Gave their all.

We are an illustrious and very prominent family.

Isadora Boggs, Sally's cousin, confided that her little sister, born after Caroline Boggs, died in infancy.

Tramped to death in the cradle by a Negro girl!

Well then.

Negroes born in Callaway are baptized and brought up Christian.

But the gross bestiality and rudeness of their manners, the variety and strangeness of their language, and the weakness and shallowness of their minds render it impossible to make any progress in their conversion.

Did I give evidence against Father?

I had no evidence to give.

He read to me.

After reading to Coffee.

He would lie in my bed and read *The Tempest*.

Or Charles Dickens.

Then I slept. Sniffing the air as if hunting for ghosts.
Dreaming of sailing on a ship of bones.
It was clear as a hallucination.
We're all deformed.
I woke up thinking,
We're all contortionists. In our own way.
We're all peculiar, flawed, crippled souls.
Orphans, exiles and outcasts.
Seeking divine redemption.
Might as well look like an angel then.
Like a heavenly body.
Even that man with one arm and no teeth.
He's an angel of the Lord.
Wolves, angels, lowlifers and sinners—bless them all.
Children of Christ Almighty.
Even the depraved are scrutinized and humiliated.
O, when the demons beguile me, filling my heart with fear
and loss,
I dream of pinnin' myself a new dress.
Lavender-ribbed silk.
Linen lining. Silk sewing thread.
Violet-colored.
Corset with whalebone.
Skirt like an inverted umbrella.
With a kaleidescope of pleats.
Complimenting the delicacy of polonaise fashion.
Not like the trucked-up skirts of the dairy maid.
I say, Let's trim the bodice with satin scallops, neatly done.
This petticoat is quilted with a splendor of spiky flowers
and swags.
Celia stitched it.
Satin face seamed then layered with woolen batting from
our own sheep.
Celia mended my cloak.
Whipstitched the edge.
Mine has a mantelet, arm slits and a pelisse.

I went to Premelia's shop in St. Louis. Bought magenta, cobalt, rose, olive, chocolate, crimson and viridian cotton.
Yellow-spotted and flowered patterned satin. And blond silk lace.
What?
These stockings were knitted by Celia.
With coral-colored silk thread.
Decorated at the ankles with clocks.
Embellishments of decorative embroidery.
Mine have a scrolling floral pattern in deep blue.
Garters above the knee and a hole worn in the bulge of the calf.
Those stockings are judged to be equal.
If you are compelled to want a woman's character.
Her disposition or integrity.
Maybe even her soul.
Take a hard and scurrilous look at her socks!
I fear to find a mysterious dust on my stockings.
Dirt from Father's grave?
O beloved Father.
The truth is mighty and must prevail.
Celia is despised.
May she be banished from this dominion forever.
What a wretched and hateful day.
This disgraceful and sickening tragedy has cut me to the bone.
How undignified.
My hair is a cyclone. A swallow's nest.
I am in a constant state of agitation.
Celia, I said. You are a trashy Negro whore.
A strumpet.
Dumber than a bag of hammers.
She insisted he had "layn" with her.
Allegations at diverse places and diverse times.
With abundance of other very gross and scandalized terms.
I had no knowledge of it.

It came like a poke in the eye with a sharp stick.
I'm a sarcophagi.
White and polished on the outside,
bloated cadaver inside. I am in a smelly state of decay.

ULYSSES a.k.a. UNCLE PEE WEE   *Old enslaved man of color. 75 years old. Bug-eyed. Gray-white 'fro with a few twisted braids. Insane inmate of Fulton State Lunatic Asylum. Committed by James S. Rollins, founder of the University of Missouri, slaveholder and guardian.*

A mute character who doesn't speak. Acts out an entire story.

Being shackled, flogged, sold on auction block, slave insurrection, transported to Missouri, mistreated and severely abused.

Silent opera. Mime. Extreme physicality. Pandemonium. Brutality. A journey. 4.5 minutes.

COFFEE WAYNESCOT *11 years old. Robert Newsom's grandson. Virginia's son. Lives in the main house. He unknowingly helped Celia spread his grandfather's ashes on the path Sunday morning, June 24, 1855.*

It's an abomination!
A detestable thing!
No, siree.
I'm not wearin' no suit.
I ain't gettin' slicked up in starchy clothes fer a hangin'.
Mother say, Make yer dead granddad proud.
We're going to Callaway courthouse tomorrow to see that rope hitched 'round Celia's neck.
Ma say good riddance to bad rubbish.
Got to pay for what she's done.
Brought shame and sorrow upon this family.
Oh my Lord!
Yeah, we got to go down there.
Well, I should be sellin' tickets.
All tickets please!
We got a carnee'val ready to start.
Billy's bringin' buckets of cat parts, cow dung and bloody innards.
Frankly, I feel ill-natured and contemptible 'bout it.
Rather be huntin' squirrels, rabbits or wild turkeys.
I got a good goin' over.
Comb your hair. Use some grease, boy!
You looks like a thistle in the wind.
Stand up straight.
Stop carryin' on like a wild cat!
Jingo say Grandpa was fornicatin' her.

Well, he was havin' carnal relations with Celia.
Don't know 'bout that exactly.
I ask Mother.
I read in the paper there was a *r-a-p-e*.
Asked her if she could explain.
She say, James Coffee Waynescot!
Shut yur trap!
You're on your way to the bottom of hell.
Demons and damnation.
Wash yer mouth with lye.
Mortifications of the flesh.
I cain't arbitrate family squabbles.
I was scared 'cuz mother was vexed.
Acting nervous and hysterical.
Havin' weak spells.
So I ask Jingo.
He say slavery is the greatest evil on earth.
And this here was a tragic entanglement of the races.
If I were a slave, I would keep tryin' to get away.
Or I'd do something real bad.
Atrocious. So then the slavers would just kill me.
Then I would just be wiped out.
Thrown to the dead chicken grave.
Truth is, I miss Grandpa. He was readin' me a story 'bout a
Cap'tain Ahab, who gets swallowed by a whale.
And Celia always come 'round with a kind word.
She could catch fireflies. Dig worms. Make turtle soup and
creamed 'possum served with coon fat gravy.
I was livin' in Grandpa's house when he died.
Got woke up by our rooster.
Roosters do not crow only at sunup.
Truth is, they crow anytime they damn feel like it.
Excuse me for swearin'.
Only thing that can be said with certainty is that they sure
do crow in the mornin'.
Was my job to throw scratch, give 'em water.

Do we need another rooster?

'Cuz the rooster has nothin' whatsoever to do with the hen
layin' her eggs.

It seems to me, actually, the hens are better off without a
rooster to harass them.

Ducks too.

I seen our sheep chased for miles by the ram in ruttin'.

Ewes not merely chased, but battered to death.

One ram climbs on, another charges and knocks him off.

Then the poor sheep gets eaten by buzzards.

A major tragedy.

And take the beewolf.

Beewolves are solitary wasps that hunt other bees and
wasps.

The males cluster together.

Each defending a small territory.

Females take a grisly revenge for unwanted attention.

It's a fate worse than death.

He'll be stung until he's paralyzed, but not dead.

Then the grubs will eat him alive.

Another disaster.

Grandpa was readin' to me 'bout all kinds of critters.

I's learnin' 'bout parasitic fig wasps.

Scorpions.

Mealworm beetles.

White-lipped land snails.

Madagascar hissin' cockroaches.

Great land crab.

Soapberry bug.

And promis'cuty in female chimpanzees.

Back in June, I was the last one to see him.

I was up in the cherry tree.

Morning Grandpa was missing.

Celia said she give me two dozen walnuts if I would carry
the ashes out.

I said, "Good lick! Yes, siree."

I put them ashes alongside the path, beat down like.

I saw Uncle Harry picking up bones out of the ashes.

I got the ashes out of the cabin she lived in.

Mother started screamin' that they were Grandpa's bones.

I'm not so sure.

See I found a pile of bones down by the creek.

I found two hooves and I think I found the legs of a deer.

I've also found something that look like a skull.

In back of the woods, I found 'em.

Scattered all over the place.

I'm still going back collectin' them one by one.

I've got about 32 total.

The biggest is probably a foot and four inches.

And the littlest one is about two inches.

The skull might be a 'coon or somethin'.

Yep.

I'm a bone collector.

Did you know, last year, a pal'ontologist found the remains of a dinosaur at the confluence of the Judith and Missouri?

Triceratops skull and fourteen tailbones.

Right on the Missouri, upriver from here.

Say it died out 65 million years ago.

Weighed three to four tons.

Was as big as an elephant and had one thousand small serrated teeth.

Them bones is the remains of prehistoric life.

A thin red line of time.

Geo'logical time.

We *Homo sapiens*—that's another word for humans.

Is just 450,000 years old.

Volcanoes is older.

But you know, rocks, they's ancient.

Older than my grandma's toes.

Three million nine hundred thousand years old.

Them's the oldest rocks known to mankind!

SOLACE *Runaway slave. Street griot.*

You know that for a fact?
That all you got to say?
What 'chu got?
I'm waitin' on somebody. Yeah.
Get! Get! Get! Get! Get out!
We gonna take all you smack devils down.
What are you? A Viking?
Neandrathal?
Contemptuous.
Ditch-scum.
I know your kind.
I know you blaspheming.
I would not be sittin' here.
You could be a witch.
I got no problem with dat.
You not going to find what you lookin' for here.
Naw.
I've been waiting to say this since 1855. Ten years before
the war.
You ever been hog-tied? Lynched? Tortured? Raped? Cas-
trated?
Sellin' children is legal. Rape is legal.
Killin' slaves is legal.
I'll cut you up. Chop feet and toes off.
Put your head in a vice.
It's a racket.
Did you steal that child?
Throw 'em into a dungeon, shackled.
Why this case?

It is a routine matter. Prevalent.
Spirits? Yeah. I believe in spirits.
Saw one with a bloody stub.
No one knows if they buried her.
She had long hair and yellow teeth.
Was wearin' a tore-up weddin' dress.
No eyes.
Her spirit would not behave.
Amputated.
No one knows.
Coonass crackers.
Bitch slut.
That mulatress got into a hog-hair scrape.
You want some? Here.
My grandmother was from Missouri.
Arkansas River Valley.
Dat's when white people made a mess.
Built a democracy based on slavery.
Constitution was written by slaveholders.
Dat's why my people are always so careful with white folks.
Celia killed a man.
You don't believe it?
Her heart was all rotted.
Apples and women both rot.
Ripped out and twitchin'.
People say she stabbed him 96 times.
Chopped him up into little pieces.
Prob'ly drank his blood.
Found the buttons from his breeches.
Found his bones.
Not the body.
Celia be dead tomorrow. 2 pm.
Ever once in a while people 'round Fulton say they see her.
That she jail break and livin' in the wet corn.
No burial rites.
No prayer for the deceased.

This is makin' me want to drink.
You want some?
She was bullyragged. A victim of injustice.
Sold. Raped. Jailed. Tried and convicted.
At the hands of Callaway County court.
All fish-belly whites on dat jury.
All twelve slaveholders.
Every one of 'em.
Dat slick counterfeit bootlicker, Abiel Leonard.
Supreme Court justice.
New Englander.
Circuit Court judge Augustus Hall too.
Hall went to Yale.
Leonard at Dartmouth.
Admitted to the bar in 1819, just before Missouri's entry
into the Union.
Well he killed a man. Yep.
A duel. Stabbed So-and-So to death.
After the Missouri General Assembly declared it to be
murder.
Got fined and reinstated.
Murderers. Thieves. Rapists. All churchgoers. Landowners.
Family men.
Jameson, Boulware and Kouns.
Didn't have any power.
Judge got all the power.
Hangin' is the real horror.
Six thousand folks come out gawkin' and hecklin'.
You ever had your back broke? Been whipped? Shot at?
Threatened? Choked to death?
You ever birth the child of your rapist?
More than once?
Should be a reenactment of the crime.
With witnesses.
Can't send a pregnant woman to the gallows.
Nope. Against Missouri law.

This is killin' me.
Man, look.
There's more than a story that's here.
No stay of execution.
That's a delay.
Just for the record.
I got a lot of stories.
I'm keep 'em all to myself.
One more thang.
That baby wasn't dead.
Listen up.
Twelve man white jury.
Juror number one. Foreman William J. Selby.
Forty-six-year-old justice of the peace from Cedar Township.
Son of a Methodist preacher. Farmer with real estate and
livestock.
Who else?
William Givens.
Stephen Gilbert.
William Lloyd.
Thomas Pratt.
John Culbretson.
William Craig.
W. J. Ficklin.
William P. Selby.
George Hossman.
Samuel Maties.
And Benjamin Sheets.
Hellfire riptide of repugnant, morally offensive men.
A violence monopoly.
Shit, that ain't nothin'.

DAVID NEWSOM   *Robert Newsom's son. 22 yrs. old. Grew*
up with male slave George as his pal.

Sister was ringin' the cowbell.
Thought there was a problem with the chickens.
She said, "Father was killed!
He's dead."
I said, "Are you sure?"
Never had cause to suspect Celia.
Harry wrote the *Fulton Telegraph* a letter
about erroneous identification of the crime scene.
Was appalled the paper stated the murder took place in the
main house kitchen.
He clarified that the Negro cabin
where the murder and burning of his body
took place is fifty yards from the main house.
In justice to the family
asked they please print a correction.

Pause.

When my older brother William died in 1835,
my cousin Ira Jarret took me and my dog Feisty into the
big room
and said, "There is yer poor little dead brother."
I recollect Jake and Conway when hung in Fulton for the
murder of
Colonel Israel Grant in 1836.
Do recall when I was five years old,
walking among the ripening wheat
which grew on the ridge

east of the house.
The Negro boy George was with me,
who is my same age.
Father was playing his banjo.
We were singin' and going fishin'.
Now George has run off.
Celia will be hanged.
And Jingo, our hog man, got rebellious.
Father sold him to Jo Saufley of Saline County for one
thousand dollars.
Gave me the money when I married this past June.
Just two weeks before his death.
Hell, we're a pioneer family.
The word with us all is—
Onward.
The hardships we have undergone
only sharpen us for the journey.

AUNT WINNIE   26 years old. Slave of Jesse Stephenson,
St. Louis, Missouri. See Library of Congress photo. Enters with
an accordion.

Aunt Winnie plays her diatonic button box for the pre-show,
with Vine while she sings her two songs or as a solo. Missouri
19th-c. jig or reel. Fiddle, banjo or spoons can be used as backup.
Also during the final scene when Celia is hanged.

JUSTICE ABIEL LEONARD   *Born in Vermont, 1797.*
Educated at Dartmouth. Trained in New York law office. Attorney. Missouri Supreme Court justice. Slaveholder. Married with children. Going through legal papers as he speaks, waiting for tailor.

Cyrus Adams versus Glasgow Steamboat.
Addicks Van Dusen & Smith versus Allen & Hickman.
Boggs versus Coleman.
Suit concerning sale of a diseased slave.
The settlement of an estate.
Case concerning overflow of sewers in Columbia.
Suit for fraudulent transfer of property.
Inheritance issue.
Slave's suit for freedom.
Settlement of Welch estate.
Suit concerning fraudulent claim of insolvency.
Adultery.
Mortgage foreclosure.
Lists of slaves sold and purchase prices.
Alleged hog stealing.
Impeachment proceedings.
Other cases relating to debt collection, manumission,
land transactions, estates, deposition concerning an
indentured twelve-year-old,
mistreatment and death of a female slave,
the rape of a schoolgirl,
a prenuptial contract,
case of fatal spousal abuse,
an estate list, replevin suit,
and will.

Here we are. File #4496.
State of Missouri versus Celia, a Slave.

Pause.

I have been tenacious to
disseminate the facts.
The nature of the issues involved are not
complicated.
She, the defendant, committed a high crime.
Confessed to it.
Willfully and with corrupt intent.
Judge Hall presided.
Jury brought a judgment against her.
Guilty of
murder in the first degree.
The conduct of the transaction in which they,
Newsom and the slave girl, had been engaged
is not permissible evidence.
As she confessed herself guilty.
To be worthy of punishment.
To take the noose.
Judge correctly bestowed a decision.
Honesty and wisdom must be correct
for the spirit and genius of our government
to flourish.
All others are sycophants and scavengers!
Do you see my silk handkerchiefs?
My tailor has arrived to
fit this new suit of expensive black cloth.
Tonight is an extravagant gala,
the Campbells' Christmas dinner.
May God bless.

MATT   *10-year-old slave boy on Death Row. Small, underfed, living in the brush. Celia's cellmate from July until November. Sentenced to death for the murder of a three-year-old white child, Virgil Wommack, Callaway County, 1855.*

Don't be an old croaker!
I got jailed. An' back-slanged.
'Cuz dey found Lil' Virgil in the blackberry bushes.
He stop breathin' and lost his brains.
Someone drag him 100 yards from the tobacca patch and mash him into pieces.
Like a dyin' animal.
Collar dat boy!
He a high-prize murderer.
I got bully-ragged. Tortured.
Accused of killin' Baby Virgil.
Miss Steel, dat Danish golddigger old maid.
She got a pickax for a nose.
Say she saw no violence in me.
Say I ain't no sugar bowl.
But ain't no ignorant ragadang.
I ain't shady.
At times I'm a friv'olous prankster.
Right now, I'm a bit grumpy.
And smell like an old saddle blanket.
No matter how you twist it up.
It's a gross falsehood.
A com'plicated mess.
Began 9th of July.
I belongs to da Hollands.
But workin' for the Steels.

Steels sent me to next farm.
Da Wommacks.
Borrow a singletree. Wood bar with metal ends.
Went to the stable to get the pry bar.
And tall hog at the trough, Sam Wommack come to get
water for the horses.
Lil' Virgil, he's 'bout three.
He's taggin'.
I's holdin' his hand.
Sam said, Matt, you get whipped if you take Lil' Virgil to
da stable.
But he jes' on me like glue.
Den, dat same afternoon, the father, Allan Wommack,
come to the Steels.
Askin' me questions.
I said I put Lil' Virgil through the gate.
I said again I left him by the white oak, next to the gate.
Wommack said he found da chile dragged 200 yard from
the house, lyin' in the fence.
Dat his head and face was cut.
Mangled in a desperate manner.
Dragged from the tobacca patch.
Thought I had hit him in the head.
Next day, tenth of July, Wommack came and took my
clothes, said they found a drop—a speck of blood.
Den I said, Lil' Virgil fell from da fence.
I throw a rock at the crow's nest and the rock hit 'em.
Dey said, You better tell the truth.
The whole truth.
Wommack tied a rope 'round ma neck.
Made it real tight.
Drew me up four or five times.
Kept yellin' and I was scared
I was gonna die.
Ma neck a piece of taffy.
Ready to snap.

Dey said I hit Lil' Virgil three times with the pry bar.
And drag him to the white oak tree.
Den said I hit him three times with a rock.
Want to kill him for "devilment."
Other white man, Craighead, took me to Wommack's
tobacco barn.
Tied me.
Strip me naked and give me 300 lashes.
Ah had blood oozin'.
Kept yelling, Say the truth, you vermin.
Flat-nosed, bullet-headed, kinky-headed culprit.
Dey kept interrogatin' me and then took me to da Fulton
jail.
I's in a cell with Celia.
On 11th of August, Baby Virgil died.
All them white men show up yellin'.
Quit beatin' da devil 'round the stump.
Dey chuckleheads. Railroad big bugs.
Ah'm afraid dey slaughter me into sausage.
So I confess to da killin'.
I's charged with first degree murder.
Da judge, pros'cutor, defense and doctor—all was same as
Celia's.
Ma trial was 4th of October.
Jury was all white mens.
Den Wommack and Craighead who hung me up and
whipped me
Admit my confession was tainted.
By the fact dey torture and almost kill me.
No person can be compelled to be a witness against hisself.
Dey brought in da pry bar.
Say it was the murder weapon, a big rock, my shirt with a
speck of blood.
Judge Hall ruled sayin' I would hang.
Well I was mad as hops.
I was scared.

I thought dey would torture me again.
Here, mobs lynch slaves like flippin' hotcakes.
Sheriff say I am guilty of murder.
Sentenced and will hang. 16th of November.
Same day as Celia.
On 15th of November, Celia and me broke out.
I heard she was brought back. Harry Newsom, drunk as a
half-rat, bring her back.
Dat's dat.
Ain't nothin' I could do.
My skiff ain't sunk.
I live wid the snakes and skunks.
I ain't a runner.
I surely ain't.
I'm bushwackin'.
Celia?
She pure as crystal.
Sang like a church bell.
Called her my woodpecker star.
She say there is a spirit inside of me and it knowed every-
thing.
But she lost dat baby.
Right here in the jail.
I seen it.
Sheriff sold it.
Den she crazy. Spun out.
Like somebody stole her rudder.
She turn mean as an old Turkish whore, cryin' all the time.
Blood everywhere.
Grit her teeth at night.
Alone like a she-wolf.
We had a spider,
You know, little pet spider.
Named her Cleopatra.
Even Cleopatra bring her no joy.
I say, Celia,

Freedom ain't somethin' you can hold on to.
Weepin' may endure for night,
But joy comes in the mornin'.
Behold the raven.
For they sow not.
Neither do they reap.
Nor gather into barns.
Yet your heavenly father feedeth them.
Consider the roses
and lilies of the field.
How they toil and spin not.
Yet Solomon in all his splendor
Was not arrayed like one of these.
Ye of little faith
Be encouraged.
Hold on, girl, hold on!

WILLIAM POWELL *41-year-old neighbor to the Newsoms.*
Farmer, slaveowner. Married with 12 children.

You'd know if he were dead, wouldn't you?
This was a fiendish, grizzly murder.
Newsom was savagely beaten and burned.
Where's our standard of decency?
As long as I live,
niggers are gonna stay in their place.
They ain't gettin' their freedom and justice where I live.
They ain't goin' to school and learn to read and write.
They ain't gonna vote where I live.
If they did, they'd control the government.
And when a nigger even gets close to a white woman, he's
tired of living.
I'm likely to kill him.
And now we got a colored girl accusin' her master of stump
grindin'!
He clean his plow?
She say she killed in self-defense.
Don't go wakin' snakes.
Jesus Christ and God Almighty.
She don't know dung from wild honey.
I was at Newsom's house, fourth Sunday in June, 'bout ten
o'clock. On the Sabbath.
I stood there and listened to Celia throw that old snot at
me.
And I made up my mind.
Pray for redemption, girl!
I'm tired of your kind stirring up trouble.
Get down on your knees and you say to God:

I was wrong!

I am sorry.

I am guilty.

I am a filthy, vicious nigger bitch.

Goddamn you.

I'm going to make an example out of you.

Just so everybody can know how the citizens in Callaway
stand.

Robert Newsom lived in this county.

Came overland, raised twelve children, cultivated this land,
was widowed and lost his life.

She is reaper's property.

This was a deliberate taking of an innocent life.

An act of derangement.

A mind infested with rats and worms.

Forgive my enemies?

There ain't no moral consideration here.

Haven't you read the book of Genesis?

This is part of God's plan.

For those darkies to serve us.

It's their destiny.

I am a servant of the Lord willing to execute wrath on the
wrongdoer.

Paul's Epistle to the Romans. Chapter Thirteen.

I went to the cookhouse where Celia was.

She wouldn't talk.

Said, You are guilty of a horrendous crime.

You made a bad choice.

George has run off.

Did he advise you to kill him?

'Fess up, girl!

George said enough to make me believe she knew where
Newsom was.

She denied it.

Said she knew nothing about him.

I said, You better tell!

Speak the truth, girl!
It will save yer neck.
I'll rip yer tongue out!
I will take your children away!
She was outright lyin'.
She still refused to confess.
I kept tauntin' her with threats.
Slammed the walls.
Broke the furniture.
Got out my rope.
It's your ass or mine, girl!
At last, she broke.
Said he had come to the back window and that
she had struck him.
He fell back outside.
And that she saw nothing more of him.
Refused to tell anything more.
But then she asked if I would send the two men—Harry
and David, Newsom's sons—out of the room.
They went out back.
And she switch the story.
Said he came into the cabin.
Think she said he came to the door.
She said she struck him twice.
Used a stick. 'Bout the size of a Windsor chair leg.
Skull-splitter.
Became alarmed. Said she was afraid she would lose her
children.
Be hung for it.
Sat there for an hour lookin' at the body.
Thought she would try to burn him.
Got a pile of wood and laid it in the fire.
She had made threats.
Threatened to hurt him on the condition
he would not leave her alone.
She said she had told the white family.

Said she threatened she would hurt him if he did not quit
forcin' her while she was sick.
I did not know that she was pregnant.
Judge from her appearance that she was.

Pause.

It was an act of treachery.
She scrappy and mad enough to murder a big white man!
What *is* the world coming to?
There was no gun involved. Could not find any evidence by
the windowsill.
No blood splatter. No witnesses. No body.

Pause.

I was there when the bones were found.
Just the buttons where she stash 'em. Bone fragments. And
his knife.

Pause.

Naw. I got no reservation about executing a juvenile.
Killin' is killin'.
I was mad enough to swallow a horn toad backwards.
Why a trial and due process?
It's just a legalistic quagmire.
Newsom's been taken from us.
A brave and honest man. My friend for thirty-five years.
He is irreplaceable. Cannot compare him to ordinary men.
Give him dignity.
That's all I ask.
When the wicked are slain,
dogs will lick the blood.

GEORGE   *22-yr.-old enslaved male. Celia's lover. Lives on Newsom farm. Bought by Robert Newsom at age five. Grew up with David Newsom, Robert's 22-yr.-old son.*

They all came at me.
I's impli'cated.
Dey all cranked up.
Drag me to da governor.
Ask dat Celia be pardoned.
What Celia done, I ain't never said a word 'bout it.
She a stray cat in a storm.
A raw-boned girl. Glazed sugar.
Ain't no expert on precious stones, but she a jewel.
Newsom, old troll lookin' for a honey pot.
I was a hazard. Left her undone.
You know. Infiltrated.
He reckless with the whip.
Guilty of a multitude of sins.
Had dreams to flatten him. Deci'mate him.
She caught, like a dark sweet bird in a trap.
Massa carried a gun. And a knife.
I say, Quit that old man.
They better shoot me first.
She say I wasn't there.
I say, She-e-e-et, you ever heard of a colored girl killin' her master?
Where you from?
Where you from?
Newsom is my white folks.
He own me for seventeen years.

Ah built the main house. Cow barn, ferrow barn for hogs.
Fences, smokehouse, slave cabin.
Milked the cows, tack dem horses, feed de hogs 'n sheep.
Oversee *eight hundred* acre. Built that chicken coop.
Yes, damn chickens. Celia. She name 'em.
Peaches. Caramel. Cap'tain Trousers. Heliotrope. Goosey.
Bearded Lady.
Cranky cock will have a mean streak.
Does a little dance for da hens.
Struts around.
Beats its wings. Real loud.
It ain't wise to have more cocks than hens runnin' in the
same pen.
Knowin' what I mean?
Shit.
That'll be that.
Dey fight fierce-like.
Nothin' like fresh eggs and fried chicken.
But . . . hell!
You're forcin' me out.
Understand?
Young cock will kill an old rooster.
Eat it alive.
Peck it to death.
A massa'cre.
You can't ever let on who did the actual killin'.
Ain't it his?
Yup, ain't it.

Pause.

Married?
No'm.
I ain't married.
Slaves not allowed to have weddings like white folks.

Ain't allowed to work for pay. Can't plant corn, peas, or
rice.
Keep hogs, cattle, horses.
Have land. Or your own name.
Slaves can't vote.
Serve on a jury.
Own or operate a boat.
Can't read books.
Carry a weapon or leave the farm.
Visit another plantation.
Evading capture is cause for whipping.
Then branded on the right cheek.
Cut your ear off. Chop yer foot off.
I wouldn't be sittin' here.
You understand?
Naw.
I sits alone at night.
My soul is stained.
Would cut my shame from me.
I mean it.
I 'bout half a man.
I would have nothin' to do with her until she quit Old Man
Newsom.
He was forcin' her.
He squander her ripeness.
It was unforeseen.
Ill-fated.
Watchin' the old man roamin' 'round her—yelling.
Demandin'. Leavin' her cryin'.
One winter, I was so cold I 'most turn white.
Celia set me before the fire. Poultice me with sliced turnips.
Didn't have 'nough clothes to keep me warm.
So she give me a blanket to bury my heart.
I make her some shoes.
She make me squirrel pie with dumplins an' rabbit gumbo.
I dance the pigeon wing and da puzzle jig.

Sang da shoofly.
Tell her stories 'bout that old gin between Saline and Jefferson.
It haunted with spirits of kilt niggers.
She take hair, brass nails, thimbles, needles and mix 'em up in a conjure bag.
I never tried the conjure.
But she keep that bag.

Pause.

I say, Celia I wants thirteen children.
A house next to the river.
Pretty water.
Warm air.
Azaleas. Tulips. Green oaks in the springtime.
Bullfrogs. Whip-poor-wills.
Smell honeysuckles and a yellow moon.
I'll build a log house. Wid chinkin', planks, sills, block, sleepers and shingles.
We raise sheep, sweet potatoes and corn.
Catch turtle.
Ride a keel down the Missouri with alls our thirteen children.
Even gots their names picked.
Cornelius, Sassafras, Eliza, Pickett, Cinnamon, Olaf, Amarillo, Lulu Mae, Jeremiah, Rufus, Oscar, Wade and Wild Cat.
You make 'em overalls with brass buttons.
Then Newsom took a whip to her. Left her by the river.
Said he would kill her. Sell her children.
He hotter than a hundred hells.
Yeah.
He got what he wanted.
He say, "Havin' a good time, ain't ya?"
Two hundred lash this time.

Split my back wid da cowhide.
So I follow the pig tracks.
Stake out.
See all these mixed-race children.
No proper retribution.

Pause.

You what?
A nigger accused of lookin' at a white woman?
What'd I just say?
Castration.
You a dead man. Dis'membered.
Hanging like a beast. Fed to the hogs.
A disgrace.
It needs sayin'.

Pause.

Naw, I ain't lookin' back.
Ah got spit enuf to drown a dog.

DR. HOCKLEY YOUNG   *One of three doctors called by the*
state to testify at Celia's trial.

Upon oath,
from the evidence,
I believe the remains of the human body now before us
are the bones and ashes of the body of Robert Newsom.
The corpus delicti, or fact of death,
is without a doubt
the bones of an adult human.
Yes, a man could be destroyed by burning
in a common fireplace between the hours of ten o'clock at
night
and four o'clock the next morning.
It would depend upon the size and heat of the fire.
Without examination of the entire burnt corpse,
the exact circumstances of the death are unclear.
However, these portions of the pelvis, skull and teeth are
still recognizable
as human.
In an actual cremation chamber, for legal incineration,
temperatures reach
2100 degrees Fahrenheit or 1100 degrees Celsius.
The body is engulfed in constant flame until it is reduced to
ash.

Pause.

Frankly, I'm more versed in the deliberate burning of pig
corpses.
Common here in Callaway and Boone.

And you can completely burn a baby in fifteen minutes.
A human adult limb burns more like a tree branch.
The thin outer layers of skin fry and begin to peel off.
Rapid tissue damage ensues.
As flames dance across the surface, the thicker dermal layer of skin
shrinks and begins to split,
Allowing the underlying yellow fat to leak out.
Body fat is a fuel source, but it needs clothing or charred wood
To act as a wick.
Human body is 90 percent water.
Water can't burn, so flesh will not actually catch fire.
The clothes will catch first.
And hair catches fire easily.
The body can sustain its own fire for approximately seven hours.
What remains is ash. And bone fragments.
Smell is terrible.
I know of two gentlemen.
One died from falling into a chimney fire.
The other man fell into a furnace.
Both died almost instantly.
Body burnt to a husk within minutes.
People tend to survive having hands and feet burned off,
unless they bleed a lot or the burn gets infected.
Suffocation and combustion are factors.
Fire has a long history as capital punishment
for saints, criminals, witches and slaves.
Joan of Arc was condemned to death.
Burned.
Fire's been used as an execution method for treason,
heresy,
malevolent witchcraft,
sexual deviancy,
incest,

homosexuality,
adultery and prostitution,
theft of sacred objects from the church,
and rebellious acts by slaves.
Last witch in Scotland was burned alive in a tar barrel in
1727.
In New York State, in 1853, two years ago,
thirty-six Negroes burnt alive for plotting a slave revolt.
Rest of them were hung.

VIRGINIA WAYNESCOT   *36 years old. Robert Newsom's daughter. Born March 23, 1819. The 4th of Newsom's 12 children. Lives in the main house with her four children, Coffee, 11 yrs., Thomas, 9 yrs., Amelia, 6 yrs., Billy, 4 yrs.*

"Shut your mouth!"
"Open your ears!"
"May as well stick my thumb up my arse and whistle."
"You ugly as a hatful of assholes!"
That's what Mother used to say.
Don't be a bother an' talk her off a cliff.
Elizabeth Betsy Gwinn Newsom. Born February 22, 1791.
In Greenbrier, Virginia.
She married Father on March 30, 1812.
She was not persnickety.
No. They rode west in an oxcart drawn by
one blind horse.
Rainin' for days like a two-cunted cow.
Then, snow ass-high on a tall Injun.
And cold enough to freeze the balls off a brass monkey.
Ma was not a lovely maiden with strawberry curls and
violet eyes.
She was forty miles of bad road.
Could pound a piano in church.
Slaughter a hog.
Discipline an errant child.
And mean enough to hunt bear with a switch.
It was an arduous and treacherous journey.
Unbeknownst to me.
I was a one-year-old baby pioneer.

Named after the state of Virginny.

Facin' every drop of travail and hardship from Lick Creek to
Callaway.

Our wagon, loaded with a hat rack, sewing machine,
walnut bookcase, parlor carpet, silver-plated pitcher, pickle
stand, kitchen cupboard, wallpaper, cookstove, farm tools
and a chickory upright.

This is the place to find God, Ma said.

And spiders, rattlesnakes, ravenous grizzlies, Injuns, hurri-
canes, cholera—and groundhogs.

"In Missouri," she said, "one day my soul just opened up
whole and deep."

Now this is a hideous place.

Father is dead as a doornail.

Ma must be feelin' mean as a sack full of wet cats in her
grave.

I last saw Pa in the evening, 23rd of June.

About twilight. Reading at the window.

We all went to bed.

Next mornin', he was gone.

I hunted in all the paths and walks.

Every place for him.

Looked in caves and along the creek.

This was Sunday.

Time for church.

And I found no trace of him.

Thought there's a rat that needs killin'.

Then comes Powell, red whiskers and a hairlip.

Sayin', You'd know if he were hidin', wouldn't you?

He's not a swine. He's a good chap. Ask the slaves.

Powell is callous and crude.

Sharp-minded. He kept interro'gatin' Celia.

And I felt sick implacable contempt.

'Cuz she was denyin' and silent.

A curse of the lowest rung.

A pitiful soul. Bootlip 'gator bait.
It's most terrifying that we kept a criminal here.
Right here in this house.
She confessed.
That even'ing we found the bones.
Under the hearth of her cabin.
Turned the large stone over to find them.
I found a gallus buckle from his overalls in the ashes along
the path.
I put those bones in a box.
Put them on the bureau 'til the next day.
Harry found the buttons my sister sewed on father's
britches.
Found them out in the ashes with the bones.
George found the knife.
The handle is burned black, but this is Pa's knife.
That night I saw the wind stretch over this red dirt land.
And wide flat jade-color rivers turn into an entry to hell.
I wish he had drowned in a raging torrent.
Been torn apart by a typhoon.
Afflicted with influenza.
Or picked clean by wolves.
But darkness pulled him to a gruesome death.
Celia's time is running out.
Convicted and condemned.
Daughter of Satan himself prancin' around.
I feel morose and vengeful.
Say Ma Betsy, "In times of conflict and sorrow, bake a pie."
Never cry.
Bake a pie.
Meat. Poultry. Fish or pheasant.
Or blackberry with piles of sugar.
Perfumey pears with ginger. Apples with clove.
Or butterscotch and meringue piled high.
I see Ma's eyes like two rusted nails.
Squintin'.

Grievous and cursin'.
A bottomless pit.
She stuck.
Squealing like a pig stuck under the gate.
Tryin' to escape and help out—in this perilous time.

VINE   *5 years old. Celia's daughter, born in Fulton Township, Callaway County. Offspring of rape by Robert Newsom. Left on farm with her 3-year-old sister, Jane, while Celia's been in jail for six months. Wild-looking. Unkept. Makes series of faces at audience.*

An' then they were chasing her.
She was runnin' and he.
The papa, he's a Bad Man.
And she ran far.
'Round by the creek.
And the dogs were runnin'.
And the Bad Man was yellin'.
Sound like a big ol' giant.
And they had guns.
Da Bad Man shot his guns.
And they all kept runnin'.
And Mama disappear.
The Bad Man put Mama in a chain.
So she was cryin'.
You know.
Mama was cryin'.

Silence.

Mama teach me to sing:

HOPPERGRASS SETTIN' ON A SWEET-PERTATER VINE,
SWEET-PERTATER VINE, SWEET-PERTATER VINE,
HOPPERGRASS SETTIN' ON A SWEET-PERTATER VINE
A SUCKIN' UP DAT JUICE.

'LONG COME A TURKEY GOBBLER SNEAKIN' UP BEHIN',
SNEAKIN' UP BEHIN', SNEAKIN' UP BEHIN',
'LONG COME A TURKEY GOBBLER SNEAKIN' UP BEHIN',
AN' KNOCKED HIM OFF DAT SWEET-PERTATER VINE.

Dat's all I know.

Silence.

Mama baked good 'possum. Do you know the 'possum
song?

WELL, 'POSSUM MEAT'S SO NICE AN' SWEET,
CARVE 'IM TO DE HEART;
YOU'LL ALWAYS FIND HIT GOOD TER EAT.
CARVE 'IM TO DE HEART.

Refrain. Female CAST *voices join in.*
CARVE DAT 'POSSUM,
CARVE DAT 'POSSUM, CHILLUN.
CARVE DAT 'POSSUM,
OH, CARVE 'IM TO DE HEART.

DE WAY TER COOK DE 'POSSUM NICE,
CARVE 'IM TO DE HEART,
FIRST PARBILE 'IM, STIR 'IM TWICE,
CARVE 'IM TO DE HEART.

Refrain. Male and female CAST *voices join in. Sing refrain
twice. Add fiddle and spoons.*
CARVE DAT 'POSSUM,
CARVE DAT 'POSSUM, CHILLUN.
CARVE DAT 'POSSUM,
OH, CARVE 'IM TO DE HEART.

VINE *sings solo to end of song.*
DEN LAY SWEET TATERS IN DE PAN,
CARVE 'IM TO DE HEART.
NUTHIN' BEATS DAT IN DE LAN'.
CARVE 'IM TO DE HEART.

Refrain.
CARVE DAT 'POSSUM,
CARVE DAT 'POSSUM, CHILLUN.
CARVE DAT 'POSSUM,
OH, CARVE 'IM TO DE HEART.

BENJAMIN SHEETS *Juror. Farmer, married, slaveholder, resident of Callaway County. One of 12 white male jurors on Celia's trial.*

Lady, lemme tell you somethin'.
Each man has his parasites.
Like knife-worms on the ranunculus.
That's right.
A slave cannot convict a white man of rape.
It's a damn "spurious issue."
Rape violates a man's legal right over an economic dependent.
And there ain't any place in the world for a poor, murderous nigger woman.
It's common sense.
There ain't no probable cause.
Celia. She as innocent as a rattlesnake at a square dance.
That licentious, pernicious fornicatress should hang.
And Jameson, the defense lawyer.
Slaveholdin' hypocrite.
He was grinnin' like a weasel in a henhouse.
Turnin' the courtroom into a nigger resort.
He's nothin' but a rich, overly educated, shady, belly-cheatin' gizzard.
Slick as two snails fuckin' in a five-gallon bucket of snot.
Makes us planters look unflatterin'.
I'm a man of unsurpassed dignity.
You thinkin'.
Where is that mean sunbitch from?
Oh, I'm from Callaway, down in there where the chickens fuck the hoot owls.

I refuse to eat a mile of nobody's shit just to kiss some
lawyer's ass.
I contain multitudes.
That's Walt Whitman.
You think I'm not a book-readin' man.
Well, you're like a boil on my butt.
He knew not what to say—so he swore.
Lord Byron.
When a man speaks the truth, his eye is as clear as the heavens.
Ralph Waldo Emerson.
And we are all tyrannized by the truth.
And Newsom, he was rich as 'possum gravy.
Tighter than a preacher's prick in a calf's ass.
Yep. According to the census, he own'd 800 acres of land.
Wheat, rye, corn, oat. Harvest'ed 1,200 bushels of grain per
year.
Hemp and flax too.
Owned 18 horses, 6 cows, 27 beef cattle, 70 swine, 25
sheep and 2 oxen.
His motto was, "Win gold and wear it!"
But he would steal the pennies off a dead man's eyes.
Also owned at least five male slaves.
Lemme tell you somethin' else.
Everything is a lie.
Even this story is a bunch of lies.
Swearin' on the Bible don't mean nothin'.
The truth is bent.
Crooked. Jacked up. Embellished.
A man who lies contaminates his own truth.
'Cuz no one will trust him.
His own truth is a trap.
Then you got lies and truth runnin' together.
Vice and virtue.
Truth is, havin' children is cheaper than buyin' slaves.
Can read it in the Scripture.
Abraham received concubines and they bore him children.

Doctrine and Covenants. 132:37.
In Missourah, fornication with a slave woman by a white
male is considered trespass.
An unlawful intrusion that interferes with one's person or
property.
That's Common Law of England.
Unauthorized entry upon land.
For example, I could sue hunters or birdwatchers who
intrude on my land.
But I cannot be charged with trespassing upon my own
property.
With intercourse, there ain't no criminal act here.
Ain't no crime or punishment for a white man raping a
slave woman.
It's his right under the law.
Now, if a buck would ravish my wife.
Rape a white gal in Missourah, he's castrated and lynched.
That's immediate execution.
Ain't no laws protectin' slaves.
Slave rape ain't a crime.
This ain't no radical abolitionist bullshit.
As for slaveowners holdin' breeding wenches:
Washington owned 316 slaves.
Jefferson, 187.
James Madison, 106.
Andrew Jackson, 160.
John Tyler, 70.
James K. Polk, 149.
Zachary Taylor, over 100.
I say the Almighty created the Grand Canyon.
Not as a geological wonderment and spectacle.
Well, the biggest hole in the earth
was carved out by the Almighty Creator for one purpose.
To round up 4 million of these black savages and throw 'em
in.
And then burn 'em.

Like a grand Fourth of July barbecue.
Lemme tell you somethin'.
If you'd taken a knife and cut the human heart out of a
white man's chest.
Cut it open and held it in yer hand.
And then cut the heart out of a nigga man.
And held it out.
No one'd know which is white or which is black.
Am I right? What you wanna bet?
But Celia, sin and wickedness,
she ain't fit to live or die.
Aw, you can save the rest to grease
Your cock 'case a pig comes by you want to screw.

JOHN JAMESON *Celia's defense attorney. Three-term member of Congress. 53 yrs. old. Flourishing law practice. Former speaker of the Missouri State Legislature. Married with four children. White slaveholder.*

What trial?
It wasn't a trial!
She was lynched.
It was a mammoth spectacle.
A charade more than a trial.
A circus of injustice.
A mockery.
Carnival ride gone haywire.
A legal, unforeseeable quagmire Kouns, Boulware and I
could not excavate or navigate our way out of.
We presented Article 2, Section 29,
Missouri Statute of 1845, stating it is a crime to "take any woman unlawfully against her
will and by force, menace or duress, compel her to be defiled."
I asked the jury if they believed from the testimony that Robert Newsom,
at the time of the killing, attempted to compel her against her will,
to have forced sexual intercourse with him,
that they will find her not guilty of murder in the first degree.
May the words "any woman" in the first clause of the Missouri rape statute
concerning crimes and punishments embrace slave women as well as free white women?

Circuit Court judge William Augustus Hall presiding held
that a slave woman could not
make a self-defense argument with respect to rape.

Pause.

Slavery is a beached whale.
Ready to implode.
Missouri is a blind man dragging this old degrading carcass
around.
This system will die of annihilation.
Or like a scorpion girt by fire
eventually sting itself to death.
Nothing arouses the citizenry with such majestic and ex-
treme emotion as the American
Negro and the problem of slavery.
In 1830, British abolitionists demanded the immediate
ending of human bondage,
which led to the freeing of 800,000 colonial slaves.
But we, in this New World, have built
race and slavery into an unnatural violent social war.
The commercial architects of chattel slavery did not develop
effective controls
to maintain this institution.
White proslavery and antislavery expansionists are at each
other's throats.
Accumulated wealth and elevated social status cannot over-
come ongoing interracial conflict.
Millions of freed and enslaved blacks are classified as per-
sons with no constitutional protections.
White slaveholders do as they please.
There is no fear of penalty.
Being conscious of one's own participation in this ongoing
ruthlessness is not even a
precondition for assuming and utilizing its benefits.
The deluding passions of slavery are inexhaustible.

I vowed to extinguish the prevailing standards and defend
Celia.
I intended to save her.
I could not.
In spite of my intellect and wisdom, an awful truth tri-
umphs.
Celia will die.

Pause. Clears throat.

My daughter Elizabeth is fourteen.
Same age as Celia when she was bought by Newsom.

EUPHRATES   *A midwife and enslaved black woman. About 40 years old. Lives on Hollman plantation, adjacent to Newsom farm.*

Don't think it was meant to be.
That child died.
Was dead when I got there.
Well, it came right hard upon you.
I was at Hollman plantation on the trash gang, down a piece from Newsom farm.
It was snowin'.
Sky like a featherbird and cold as a grave digger's butt.
Look like an ice fairy tale.
Big Zack came, pounded at my door, carry me through the snow.
Whew! That night was a blizzard.
They call Dr. Cotton. He white folks doctor, but he show up two days too late.
More than a mile to the jailhouse.
And we were duckin' trees and drifts.
Celia was yellin' when we get to her cell.
I put down an old blanket and newspaper on the floor.
Put my ax next to me.
Ain't no bed. Just boards and straw.
No cast-iron pot with hot water boilin'.
It was cold. Cement and steel.
Rats, rusted nails. Jailer was a menace.
Celia was screamin'.
I stood her up.
Rubbed her with roots and herbs to calm her.
But I knew.

The blood was dark.
Purple-red.
She squat.
When I catch that baby, it wasn't movin'.
No heart beat. No cryin'. 'Twasn't breathin'.
Looked beautiful. Not dead.
She look like she's sleeping.
Only one other baby I caught with a cord around the neck.
Choked.
But this one, the heart was not working.
But it sure wuz a picture to look at.
A jewel. Gave it to her to hold.
There was only an oil lamp—an the moon shinin' in.
Oh Lord. Dat baby precious.
Skin the color of twilight and gingerbread.
Little hands. Rosebud lips. Pretty eyelashes. That lil' one
shipwrecked.
She a torn blessing. A disappointment.
But Celia broke open. Shattered. Fell into a deep well of
tears and sorrow.
Wasn't meant to be. Uh-uh.

Pause.

Da owl came to me. Two night ago.
Start screechin'. Knew somebody would die. Didn't think it
were a child.
You know, plenty of slave women have children by the
white man.
She know better than to not do what he say.
Mulatto children everywhere. White mens rape their slaves
just like they breed horses.
The massas—they proud of it.
Go with the colored women.
And then when they daughter's about 12 or 13, start with
them too.

Call em fancy girls. Quadroons, octoroons.

Over in Saline County, one white lady slipped in a colored gal's room and cut her baby's head clean off 'cause it belonged to her husband.

Celia, she know her hangin' day.

She ain't blind.

Jailer drop that baby in a coal bucket.

I shut my eyes and prayed that lil' spirit find its way back.

Back to the river and float on the shell of a mud turtle and land in the springtime on the yellow leaves of a big cottonwood.

Now, I'm *Euphrates,* da midwife.

My name comes from a river in Mes'potamia.

I will not be outfoxed.

I ain't no one to tangle with.

Now, do you believe this story?

Do you know all dis for a fact?

Well, it ain't true. What I just told ya. Nah. It's a hoax. A bunch of lies.

Dey turn dis into a circus. And vicious gossip.

That baby wasn't dead. No, Ma'am.

Judge Hall force me to keep quiet.

But ah delivered that baby. It considered a scandal.

Black girl in jail, nine months pregnant and convicted of a cap'tal crime, killin' a white man.

So dey sold dat chile.

To da white folks. Broadwaters.

Said, "How much?" Dey give da court fifty dollars.

Told me to hush up. I was there. Wrap it in rags and old piece of quilt.

Took the cord and the afterbirth, bury it under the pear tree.

Dat baby ain't in a grave. But her mama will be soon.

Accordin' to the off'icial records, Celia's third chile was stillborn.

But I'm here to tell ya.

Her name is Jennie Broadwater Newsom, born November
2, 1855. She's alive and kickin'.

That's the truth.

Listen to me good.

There's two spirits.

One good. The other evil. Troublesome.

The good spirit is heaven-bound.

The problem spirit is the "trublin'" spirit.

The trublin' spirit is disquieted.

Roams the land where it once lived, disturbin' all there.

Roamin' spirits will be attracted to tree branches.

If you put a blue bottle on a tree branch, when the sun
strikes, it causin' the glass to flash.

Glitter.

Da roamin' spirit will be trapped inside da bottle.

Some believe the first ray of the morning sun destroy the
spirit inside.

Dat unknown viper will be spooked out.

I'm collectin' blue glass bottles for Celia.

Open da gate for the spirit of Celia. She will be hanged, but
she won't be gone.

'Cuz the dead are never gone. They are here in this house.

Dey are in the trees and the grass and shadows. Nope.

Dead are right here wid us.

JUDGE WILLIAM AUGUSTUS HALL   *Circuit Court judge. Born in Portland, Maine. Attended Yale. U.S. Senator. Slaveowner. Married with children.*

If Newsom came to her cabin
on the evening of June 23rd
speaking to her about
having intercourse with her
or any other matter,
there is no damage, motive or probable cause.
The court received her confession,
which she signed with a cross-mark,
undermining presumption of innocence.
The defendant had no right to kill Newsom.
Under Missouri law,
slaves accused of capital crimes
are entitled to a court-appointed attorney.
Counsel for the defense
Jameson's claim that the Negro girl killed Newsom
unintentionally while defending herself
against rape was unfounded.
Jury deliberation determined a verdict of murder in the first
degree.
Under Section 1, Chapter 47, Revised Statutes of Missouri
1849,
the defendant was found guilty of intent to kill the deceased
as a *willful, deliberate and premeditated act.*
Subsequently,
a motion was filed by the defense
pleading the court grant a new trial.

I overruled the motion and pronounced Celia, ordered
to be executed by hanging on November 16th.

Pause.

My calculation is slavery is necessary
and barbarous.
It's a dark and turbulent *partnership*
under which it preserves the Nation's balance.
If emancipation is proclaimed,
we will experience tenfold greater evils than we ever have.
For the relief of our people,
I have concern
these acts of destruction will break forth with greater vio-
lence
than ever before.
Rebels and abolitionists are a constant annoyance in steal-
ing our Negroes!
Blacks have a "divine" relationship with enslavement.
God used the crucible of slavery to resocialize Africans.
Transform them into
respectable members of society.
Exposed to the manners and arts of civilized Christian life.
We were admitted as a slave state in 1821.
Under the mysterious providence of the Almighty,
may we remain a large, sovereign slaveholding entity.
By the grace of God, for my wife, Septimia Sebree Hall and
my beloved children,
Octavia Kasey, Anna Sonia
and baby Emma Baskett Hall, and for all of Missouri.
Now, pardon me.
We're off to the Christmas ball.

HIGGLER   *Hangman. 40-ish. Big, fat, snotty mess of a*
man. Physically repulsive. Speaks with a British accent.

Piss off!
Cowfucker!
May the bow of a violin enter your anus!
I never was squeamish.
I'm up to my neck in niggers!
Pilforin' cheaters, murderers, gut robbers!
Got smaller brains and incurable mental
disease.
You catch 'em and convict 'em.
I'll hang 'em.
Don't shite through yer teeth.
Else your ears turn into arseholes and shite on yer shoulders!
With the English,
the hangman is like the dog.
The friend of man.
Celia.
Cat piss smelling bloody cunt!
Nasty leper queen can blow my dick.
Sluice yer gob!
Here, take a drink.
Might need a shot a' tarantula juice before I set the ropes.
A bungled or botched hangin'?
There was a case where the prisoner's head
jerked right off the body.
An official decapitation.
Come unshucked.
Christ, what a mess!
Can also be groans.

Ugly spasms.
Wheezin'.
Defecation.
In 1849, there was a husband and wife hanged side by side.
Very unusual.
That was jail square, Glasgow.
Drew a crowd of about thirty thousand.
Was for the murder of the mother-in-law.
When I officiate,
the clothes and personal items of the condemned
are mine to sell.
Rope can be sold by the inch.
There is rules.
Can't pull a greasy string out of a cat's ass for a noose!
It is illegal and not likely
to hang a pregnant hussy.
In China, heads are taken off with a sword.
Ears and strips of flesh cut off.
Fried and eaten before the execution.
My great-uncle Dudley Higgler,
Cornish blue beard,
carried out over two thousand executions.
Wore a long white coat and top hat.
He was a cobbler by trade.
Sold meat pies outside Newgate on hangin' days.
Veal and pork.
Rabbit.
Trotters.
Some chicken feet.
Blood.
Heart.
Snout.
Tongue.
Tendons.
Brain.

Kidney, livers and tripe.
Well stubby, tomorrow
you can suck butter from my ass.
We're havin'
meat pie with fried nigger sausage!

FELIX BARTEY   *Callaway Circuit Court clerk.*

File #4496.
State of Missouri versus Celia, a Slave.
Callaway County Court trial expenses.
For the cost of administering justice:
Felix Bartey,
Clerk of the Court,
That is I,
am due fourteen dollars and eighty cents
for copying the indictment, issuing subpoenas, swearing in
the jury and witnesses,
entering an appeal to the Supreme Court,
and completing a case record for the court.
Sheriff William Snell, due one hundred and four dollars and
fifty cents
for summoning witnesses, the expense of boarding the
prisoner
from 25th of June for 171 days at forty cents per day,
totaling sixty-eight dollars and forty cents.
And for executing Celia's death warrant.
D. M. White, justice of the peace, due two dollars for re-
cording testimony,
issuing a subpoena and taking the oaths of three witnesses.
D. S. Whaley, due twelve dollars for providing meals to the
jurors,
who each is due one dollar and fifty cents for his services.
Witnesses at the trial will be paid a total of thirty-nine dollars and thirty cents.
Robert Prewitt, prosecuting attorney, earned a fee of twenty
dollars.

Grand total for the state of Missouri, two hundred and ten
dollars and eighty-five cents.
Judge William Hall and attorney Robert Prewitt will exam-
ine the bill of cash
and order it to be certified to the auditor of public records
for payment.
Thus has closed
one of the most horrible tragedies ever enacted in our beloved country!

CELIA *19 years old, eve of her execution, December 20,*
1855. Jail cell, Callaway County Courthouse, Fulton Township,
Missouri. She has been incarcerated since June. One eye is closed
shut. Her face is swollen. Her body is bruised and fragile. Her
mind broken and unraveled.

My dog ain't in dat fight.
You a liar!
A skank.
Devil's on top.
Devil's in da icebox.
Ain't you the one?
She step on a bullfrog.
Go piss up a rope!
Gag a maggot.
Useless slave spec'ulator.
I never was in any way dis'graced.
Scarcely know what ah'm here for.
Have no idea fer what purpose I was taken here.
Get me ready fer huntin'!
Mad enuf to chew horseshoes.
Spit nails.
Spit out a toad!
Sanctimonious
swag-bellied
chicken shit
sin and wickedness.
You a liar!
Devil's got into me.
Hatbox.
Brain-tanned.

My fault. I was born bad.
All my teeth crooked.
Crack! Crack! Crack! Crack! Crack! Crack!
Dey crossed and uncrossed.
Lost all my baby teeth.
Sold 'em.
Whose baby was hackin'?
One thing. There is several witches concealed in this jail.
Wearin' a white and red checkedy calico apron.
Under da pear tree.
I have lived to die.
Where you goin' Auntie?
I goin' to hell, I reckon.
Dey didn't care if you froze.
Swallow dat grub. Chaw it.
Buck and gag bench.
Girl, how is you feelin'?
Dis ain't even mine.
Cow's tongue.
Suck this.
Was born the year the cat crossed my path.
I mean, to grow me took a lot.
Mama July ain't survive.
She robbed in the woods.
Got yanked up.
Get out the way so I ain't killed.
Unhitched. Whipped. Killed in a scandal.
See, they count my age when I get here.
Right now, I'm astr'onomical in the numbers of age.
I'm old as the sun.
Slidin' right outta da sky.
Can't tell you.
Naw, reeky, thick-eyed ratcatcher.
It changed when dey built dis jail.
Animal cage wid guns.
I was five.

Jes' a chile.
It was a surprise. Invasion.
Dey spo-lit us up.
Pimps. Grubs. Shuckin'.
Gonna hang her to a sour apple tree.
Everybody dress up fine for dey funeral.
Don't touch de dead.
Don't let de fire go out.
Won't speak my language to anyone.
I got me a dic'tionary.
I mean, that's what I read.
That's what I write.
Dey kill you in the high church fer readin'.
Anyone kent go to my church.
Don't share my religion wid anyone.
Jes' like my own tongue and my own name.
What the matter wid you?
All spewed up wid lice?
I get re-baptized.
Knifed with rat poison.
Kill a couple hogs.
Beat to death.
We get new names when we got here.
Not allow'ed to tell anybody. Evil influence.
Like ah'm not allowed to speak my own tongue.
See, go back to day one.
Half-bloods.

Pause.

Did you hear the news?
You know?
Men kill.
Dey kill.
Did you hear the news?
Yer gun belong to someone else

On de other side of de gun.
And they *not* goin' to protect you.
I'm a cook.
Cook feet, tail, brains. 'Possum. Quail. Squirrel. Turtle.
Onion tea.
Squeeze dose innards.
Suck the marrow.
Ah done take my freedom.
'Cuz this ain't the kind of world I like.
Holy Mother of God.
Not really.
I've sacrificed ever'thing
I ever loved or cherished
or wanted to have or desired or couldn've had.
Jes' sacrificin' and givin' it up.
And give it up the way I had to.
And what it left me.
I give it to no one
that's goin' to get to keep it
forever,
'cuz dey get it in a way that they ain't goin'
to keep it eter'nally.
In da rivers of hell.
Well, I've outlived 'em.
Might say I've kind of outlived
all my greatest joys
and greatest blessings.
Ah got nothin' I had to give up
and give to dem and had to live dis life I had to live
because I had to do without
to give it to them!
'Cuz de way they chose dat, they ain't gonna *get* to keep it.
Dey gonna lose it.
De same way.
Gonna hurt 'em more than it ever hurt me.
'Cuz truth is, it ain't theirs.

Dey've ac'quired it illegally.
An intend to keep it all
illegally through an illegal legal system.
My greatest joy for years was goin' back to my chillun.
Going back and countin' da minutes and seconds
of der future forever dis'appointment.
And heartbreak.
Dey just started breakin' hearts.
And dey one of da wealthiest, holy-God-hell families in all
creation.
Der ain't nothin' that money can't buy.
I'm not worried.
Dey jes' start to break hearts.
'Cuz dat baby ain't survive.
Pick her up on the way to dis world.
She die a horrible death.
Pigs ate half her face.
You hear the screams?
I's old enough to hear all the screams.
Old enuf to know what happen.
She with me now.
I throw 'em away.
Oh God.
I've thrown em'rals, rubies,
di'mons, sapphires away.
I always have.
Mama got no pearls.
Should catch me on a mad day when ah'm throwin' jewels
'round.
Crazy.
It like the shoe that don't fit.
All my posses'ions are free to anyone.
You want my wickedness?
Even my baby teeth are free.
My holy-God-hell baby teeth.
It a long story.

You don't know Massa Newsom?
You don't even know me, do you?
Ya don't even know my history or my home or my
cir'culation.
Where are brains made?
If your brain is a jail.
A gov'nment-run jail to get away wid murder.
Put 'em in the stocks.
Head in one hole. Arm in de other.
Beat to death.
There is several witches concealed in this jail.
Grandma Pearlie, what happen?
Don't leave me alone.
Ah don't like to be inside.
Somebody just got burned fresh.
Somebody die right soon.
Don't touch de dead. Don't touch de dead. Don't touch de
dead.
Raw heads.
All spewed up with lice.
Yeah, the day I was born brand new.
Did you get skinned?
Did you get raped?
Beaten?
Imprisoned?
Impounded?
Did dey steal your chillun?
Dey split us up.
Demons got her.
White men.
Faster dan a mongoose.
Drown dat skunk.
Now they on the second half of da story.
Da ending.
For every ending, der's a beginning.
You know why for ever' ending, der's a beginning?

Well, ah quit cryin'
all my tears long time ago.
Quit screamin' all my screams long time ago.
Ah'm a burnt seed.
Dead bird.
Chopped up pieces of my heart.
Took dose pigeon wings.
Yellin'.
Ma hair.
Sew'd it on da dress.
Hides it in da heart.
Truth buried in tunnels.
In dat dress.
Death ridin' a horse.
Say ah don't want you spite
you hate, you mis'conduct or lies.
Where der is heat, der is fire.
Had ma chillun
in a big hole.
Get outta da way.
Gots to wash da stains off dis dress.
Wounds of de world.
'Cuz ah'm gettin' killed.
Don't owe you shit!
Malig'nant, ven'omous white motherfucker,
I'm gonna shank you!

Final Scene: Celia is hanged.

CELIA *Voice-over narration for film/video. Shot from Celia's point of view, handheld, Super 8 sepia tone, iPhone, hybrid surveillance video, splintered random images and 19th-c. daguerreotypes. Projected during the hanging, the final scene. Approx. 5 minutes.*

A horse can see ghosts.
A bird flyin' into a house is a sure sign of death. And never step over a swarm of snakes!
A cat should not be allowed in the room with a corpse.
And catfish bones straddle the land of the living and the land of the dead.
Plant snap peas by the light of the moon.
Plant potatoes and beets when da moon is dark.
Goose grease and honey will cure all that ails you. White onion soup and hot foot soaks too.
Ain't no good medicine like dat here.

Pause.

I was fourteen years old den.
Put up on the courthouse auction block to be sold.
Old Man Newsom not from my county.
He look ornery. Starin' at me.
When he bid, Grandma Pearlie start cryin' a bucket.
Nigger trader shove his hand in my mouth.
Den I was sold to Massa Newsom, and he put me in his buggy goin' to Callaway.

He say, "Stop that cryin'. You wench. You pretty as store-
bought sin. No whinin' or I'll beat you
'til you ugly as a bucket full of worms."
Then his face caught on fire. Like someone put it out wid
an ax.
He was lower den a snake's belly.
I was angry, but said nothin'. On the ride to Callaway, he
push me out
the wagon and I fell on the road.
Pitched and lurched under the wheel.
Said if he didn't kill me, the nigger-catchers would.
Den he raped me.
I remember a fly land on my shoulder and my arm dangling.
The clouds in the sky twist like broke chicken necks.
He caught my throat, so I could not scream.
I heard the wind scrapin' the trees.
Next day we get to Callaway, my dress was ruined and I
was bleedin'.
I heard a wimmin's voice and the children were laughin'.
Miss Polly look like a pumpkin tilt sideways. Took me to
the slave cabin.
We walk by the garden and she talkin' proud 'bout the
hollyhocks.
Gladiolas and peonies stare back at me, sweet with hate.
Nine months later I give birth to Vine. I name her after
grapevines and tomatoes.
My auntie in Audrain had honeysuckle and a climber wid
orange trumpets. What if I named her
Trumpet? Well dat a crazy name for a chile. So I settled on
Vine.
Den she crawled like a caterpillar into my heart.
One year later came Little Jane, small as a mustard seed.

Pause.

You want to know about dat night? Last June? Why you
want to know?

Newsom rape me for five years. Spoke wid his daughters,
but dey ain't do nothin'.

Dey meaner than two bulldogs in a blazin' fire.

I ain't a liar. I surely ain't. And I ain't crazy. I took sick with
another chile. Was my third.

Was smitten' with George. My heart was cast-off.

He hold my scarce and broken parts.

He smell right.

Sweet like muskrat.

But Newsom was fumin'.

Said, You cannot marry that young buck.

He push his way into the cabin. He kept grabbin' me and
laughin'.

I's pregnant. Sick. But he always do what he want.

Was drinkin'. Den he hits me. I said, Don't wake my children. He say, Don't talk to me that way.

Nobody care about them.

He start talkin' 'bout evil acts. Caught me by da throat. Got
out his knife.

His eyes got grayish—like old milk. He smell like maggots
and grease. Said, I'll split your belly and crush that baby
skull if you don't pull your skirt up.

He tries to hit me again.

My spirit was hidin'
under an old, twisted, thick-rooted muscadine bush
then tore open flappin' its wings of misery and fury.

I picked up dat hickory stick and hit 'em.

As soon as I struck him, the devil got into me.

He fell and I heard the nightbird. I didn't mean to kill 'em.

I watch all his vileness run like a river on the way to hell.

There was a sickness in him. Festered inside him like a dead
skunk.

I rolled him into the fire. Doubled him up.

Kindled the fire over and around him with hogshead staves.

Burned him up.

No I did not carve him up.

They callin' me a murderer. Black trash.

Sayin' my name like hearin' somethin' ugly. Did not chop him up. I ain't no butcher.

Next mornin', sun was up. Smilin' down upon us.

After breakfast, the bones were not entirely burnt up.

I took up the ashes. Out of the fireplace where I burnt the body.

Spread 'em on the right-hand side of the path leading from my cabin to the stable.

I ask Coffee to help me wid da ashes. I give him 2 dozen walnuts.

Jingo and Milt were totin' water to the field.

Vine and Jane jumpin' rope. Flint playin' marbles and Coffee was climbin' dat cherry tree.

I put on my calico dress, dyed indigo for church. But dem Newsoms was hysterical. In a panic.

Da sky spun upright and I saw it comin', da angel of death.

I ran. Hid in the corn dat night.

They got the bloodhounds after me. Got chewed up. One dog got my eye.

Was muti'lated and mangled.

Dey kick me until I almost dead.

Said I's gonna hang by the neck.

Said, Tell the truth, or we kill you and yer children.

Drag me to the jailhouse next mornin'.

Den I's in court fer da trial.

I tried to break out. To see my children the last time.

My third baby's gone. Had her right here.

A gal chile. Lil' hummingbird.

Jailer snatch her. Sell her to white folks.

Before dey take her, I say, Pea Blossom, there ain't no one in heaven equal to you.

There will be a time comin' when you are not a slave.

You will go to school, ride a riverboat. This time is upon us.

Remember the eyes follow the heart, over the edge of what
we cannot see. Into the darkness of
what we can only know.
Forgive me, child.

Pause.

Watch my girls. Will you watch 'em?
Keep 'em from the cold.
Keep 'em from da av'lanche of evil.
Keep 'em from the bleak, bitter and ugly.
Don't let 'em get stranded.
Give 'em homemade ginger beer. Raspberry pie and fresh
cream. Warm buttered waffles.
Give 'em books and writin' paper.
Don't tell this story.
A motherless child has got a hard time ahead.
Take 'em to the place where I'll be hung.
Go to dat place.
Don't tell this story.
Don't tell this story.

END OF PLAY

Acknowledgments

Celia, a Slave was initially read on September 8, 2015, at the Flea by the core resident company ensemble, the Bats. The first public staged reading was at the Claire Tow Theater in Lincoln Center on September 10, 2015, under the direction of Niegel Smith, who turned the play into a raw feral jewel. Niegel and I cut characters and text for the Lincoln Center event. I bid farewell to Jingo, Zachariah, Flint, and Coffee's history of Callaway County. To the cast who kicked it out of the park: Pernell Walker, Emma Duncan, Marjorie Johnson, Gayle Rankin, Calvin Dutton, Pico Alexander, Mirirai Sithole, Dave Quay, Christopher Innvar, Ronald Peet, Quincy Dunn Baker, Crystal Lucas-Perry, Kara Young, and fiddle player Josh Henderson.

Thank you to heavyweight historian and scholar John Wess Grant, who introduced me to Celia's trial in 2011. For invaluable archival and research assistance, I thank the Himmel Park Public Library staff, Missouri Supreme Court Archives, and State Historical Society of Missouri.

I am deeply grateful to Nicholas Wright, John Donatich, Erica Hanson, Christopher Rogers, Francine Horn, Jaron Caldwell and Mark Orsini. While writing, I was inspired and supported by Sydne Mahone, Darrell Wilson, Diana Herrera, Nathan Ginn, Uzo Nwankpa, Stephanie Chace, Brick P.

Storts III, Kathleen Williamson, Wendy Volkmann, Cathy
Raphael, Carol Reinhart, Josh Guy Josserand, Joe McGrath
and the impeccable Rogue Theatre, the Dunbar Coalition,
Patrick Baliani, Nicholas and Jake Seyda, James Seyda, and
my beloved parents, Alice and John.

My thanks extend to the hog farmers, midwives, attor-
neys, and the descendants of slaves and slaveowners whom I
interviewed for this project.

I am also indebted to the WPA Slave Narratives and mu-
sical genius Sam Lucas, the African American singer and
songwriter who wrote *Carve Dat 'Possum*. *Hoppergrass Settin'
on a Sweet Pertater Vine* is attributed to the Grayson County,
Virginia, fiddler Luther Davis, and based on an old African
American folk song and rhyme.

A final heartfelt embrace to "Get Around," a.k.a. Bee, who
channeled the spirit of Celia and taught me to listen.